ÈṢÙ is not satan

Exploring the Indigenous Yorùbá Worldview

Israel Ayanwuyi

2023

Èṣù is not Satan:

Exploring the Indigenous Yorùbá Worldview

For copyright permission and other related matters, please contact:
phone: +234 703 293 2463
email: ayanwuyiisrael@gmail.com
social: www.linkedin.com/in/israelayanwuyi

DEDICATION

To Olódùmarè, the Supreme Being,

Whom my ancestors have known

since time's dawn.

TABLE OF CONTENT

INTRODUCTION

How would you feel when you are given a name or identity that does not belong to you, if your true identity is submerged underneath lies and misconceptions? How could you thrive, live, or explore among people who call you names that are far from your true essence?

This predicament, this terrible situation, among other distortions has plagued Yorùbá Indigenous Practices for years, particularly spurred by Àjàyí

Crowther's wrong translation of Èṣù to mean Satan.

Yet, how can one continue to exist, to bear a name that is not truly one's? It is paramount to dispel the misinterpretations and misconceptions surrounding Èṣù, as it holds the key to fostering a deeper understanding of both the Yorùbá indigenous practices and 'Yorùbánity' (– essence of being a Yorùbá). Evidently, many Yorùbá Christians and Muslims lack a comprehensive understanding of the distinctions between Satan in the Bible or Qur'an and Èṣù in the Yorùbá pantheon.

Through meticulous and profound research, nuanced exploration of theological and cultural perspectives, this book endeavours to unveil the authentic nature of Èṣù in Yorùbá Indigenous Religion. By delving into the scriptures, traditional oral accounts, and the profound compendium of Yorùbá wisdom – Ifá, you, dear reader, are on a transformative journey that elucidates the distinct character and role of Èṣù. Likewise, the intricate web of Yorùbá culture, spirituality, and indigenous practices will be meticulously examined to unearth the profound influence that the understanding of Èṣù has had on Abrahamic religions and the Yorùbá indigenous practices today.

The misconception that Èṣù is equivalent to Satan in the Bible stems from a misinterpretation in translation of the Bible to Yorùbá by Bishop Samuel Àjàyí Crowther, who wrongly equated Èṣù, an Òrìṣà in Yorùbáland, with Satan in the Abrahamic context.

According to an account, Àjàyí Crowther was around 12-years of age when he and his family were captured from Ọ̀ṣogùn, his village near Ọ̀yọ́, by the Fulani invaders around 1821 and were sold to the Portuguese slave raiders. This incident, perhaps, caused his little knowledge, if any, of Èṣù and his role in the Yorùbá pantheon.

As Chinua Achebe wisely said, "Until lions have their own historians, the sons of hunter will always write history to glorify their hunting." This book aims to bring clarity and dispel the misconceptions that have perpetuated the erroneous equating of Èṣù with Satan. By illuminating the distinct natures of these entities within their respective religious frameworks, readers will embark on a transformative journey that transcends dogma and fosters a deeper appreciation of cultural diversity and religious harmony. Ultimately, through this exploration, a bridge shall be built, uniting Yorùbá people with the richness of their cultural heritage, and enabling individuals to embrace their faiths in their true essence while honouring the sacred heritage of the Yorùbá people.

In the past, I have published numerous articles aimed at enlightening people about the true nature of Èṣù and dispelling the inaccurate notion that equates Èṣù with Satan. I spearheaded multiple campaigns, dedicated to rectifying this misconception and fostering a proper understanding of Yorùbá Indigenous Practices. Now, I am deeply indebted to the numerous individuals who have greatly enriched my knowledge and understanding, playing an instrumental role in the creation of this book. Their contributions, both conscious and unconscious, have been immeasurable. Without their guidance, I would not possess the substantial evidence, riveting presentation, or compelling reasons to write this book, aimed at educating all those who yearn for genuine knowledge. It brings me immense joy to have you as part of this journey, as we collectively engage in the process of learning, unlearning, and relearning.

Á jú șe o!

—Israel Ayanwuyi

DIVINITIES AND THE YORÙBÁ WORDVIEW

Within the Yorùbá indigenous practices, there exists a belief system since the primordial times that revolves around the concept of *Olódùmarè*, the Supreme Being. According to this belief, Olódùmarè is not only the Creator of all things but also the sustainer and provider of life for everything, including the acclaimed various divinities. While these divinities hold a position of lesser rank in comparison to the Supreme Being, they possess their own unique origins.

Firstly, there are primordial divinities, called *Irúnmọlẹ̀* that have existed since the very beginning of time. These primordial beings are deeply woven into the fabric of existence and hold immense significance for the Yorùbá. Secondly, some of the divinities called *Òrìṣà* are revered ancestors who have been deified over time, their remarkable lives and accomplishments leading to their elevation to divine status. Finally, there are divinities that personify natural phenomena, embodying the essence and power of the natural world.

These classifications provide a framework for understanding the diverse range of divinities within the Yorùbá pantheon. Despite their varying origins and characteristics, these divinities collectively hold a revered position in the indigenous practices and beliefs of the Yorùbá people. They serve as intermediaries between humanity and the Supreme Being, playing essential roles in the spiritual and cultural lives of the community.

The worship of divinities is central to the Yorùbá belief system, where these divine beings are considered an integral part of the spiritual realm. In Yorùbá indigenous belief, *Irúnmọlẹ̀* known as primordial divinities are recognized and regarded as entities created with a significant purpose of serving the will of the Olódùmarè in the Universe. They are often referred to as 'Ministers' or 'Vassal' of the Supreme Being, with each having specific role(s) in the governance of the world.

An *Ifá* corpus (which is a compendium of Yorùbá wisdom – Also a divinatory system that contains our stories, culture, religion, science, civilization and more) elucidates this:

> *Àbàtà ńlá ni baba Ẹ̀fọ̀n wọnyí*
> *Adífá fún gbogbo ọ̀kànlénírinwó Irúnmọlẹ̀,*
> *Wọ́n tọ̀run bọ̀ wá ilé ayé*
> *Ẹbọ ogbó atọ́ ni wọ́n wá ṣe...*

\- Excerpt from ÈjìOgbè

According to Yorùbá beliefs, divinities are associated with Olódùmarè, the Supreme Being, since the beginning of creation. The Irúnmọlẹ̀, divinities such as Òrìṣà-Ńlá (Ọbàtálá), Ọ̀rúnmìlà, Ògún, Èṣù, Ṣàngó, and Ọ̀ṣun were among the earliest divinities closely connected to Olódùmarè with their interconnected roles on earth. These divinities are prominent with specific functions, recognized by the Yorùbá, and they are universally worshipped.

Exploring the origin of Èṣù may not yield specific answers from the Abrahamic religions (like Christianity, and Islam) because Èṣù is alien to them. Èṣù is an Irúnmọlẹ̀ to the Yorùbá people, and it is the Yorùbá indigenous practices that can provide explicit explanations, offer important insights and significant narratives into Èṣù's nature and character through oral traditions and Yorùbá wisdom and literatures (like Ifá).

A trusted account of Ifá (and many others) point out that after the world's creation, Olódùmarè assigned the divinities to oversee its affairs and serve as intermediaries between the Supreme Being and His creation. In Yorùbá theology, Èṣù was one of the original and primordial divinities sent by Olódùmarè from heaven to earth. Each of these divinities was endowed with specific powers and functions. For instance, Òrìṣà-Ńlá was responsible for matters of creation and governance as the eldest, while Ọrúnmìlà served with wisdom and foresight. Òrìṣà-Ńlá was commissioned to create and enrich the earth, while Ọrúnmìlà declared Olódùmarè's will to the earth, shaping it through profound wisdom and understanding of divine matters.

Èṣù, on the other hand, was appointed as the Inspector-General and chief enforcer of Olódùmarè's will on earth. He is a prominent deity who serves as the intermediary between the positive and negative forces (Ire àti Ibi) or openness and closeness (ojú àti òdì). Èṣù is the deity that checks the excessive use of power in both the physical and spiritual realms. Èṣù is the deity who serves humanity, rewarding everyone accordingly. He is a force that is not influenced by any particular options. He represents a force of balance, much like a referee in a sport.

It is believed that Èṣù is also responsible for safeguarding the power of *"Àṣẹ,"* the divine and potent power through which the divinities perform supernatural abilities. His position as the inspector-general, intermediary between heaven and earth, central intelligence officer, gatekeeper and chief law enforcer makes him prominent among other divinities. Considering the significance of sacrifice in Yorùbá practices, Èṣù's role as the carrier from earth to heaven also holds considerable weight.

The Yorùbá belief system revolves around the worship of divinities, with each divinity serving a specific purpose in the governance of the Yorùbá world. Èṣù, as a primordial divinity, was assigned the role of the inspector-general, entrusted with the responsibility of overseeing worship practices. His authority over supernatural powers and his influence over human beings and other divinities make him a prominent and complex figure in the Yorùbá pantheon. Èṣù is the chief enforcer of natural and divine laws, the orderliness and law enforcement agent of Olódùmarè on earth. Thus, to the just and upright, Èṣù is kind and good, while to the pervert and wrongdoers, he is perceived evil.

YORÙBÁ'S CONCEPT OF EVIL

In the Yorùbá worldview, the concept of evil is encompassed by the word *"Ibi,"* which carries a range of meanings. It represents anything that is unpleasant, the absence of joy or blessings, or the corruption of goodness *(Ire)*. Evil is seen as undesirable, unfavourable, and distasteful; diminishing the ideal state of life. Anything that hinders the attainment of goals, ideals, happiness, or overall well-being is considered *ibi.*

If a person dies at a young age, the Yorùbá would readily perceive this loss as evil (ibi) because it brings sorrow to the entire family of the deceased. Wherever such occurs, the Yorùbá would pray, *"Olódùmarè á dáwọ́ ibi dúró"* (God will put an end to evil). Similarly, if someone experiences a severe accident resulting in the amputation of their limbs, the Yorùbá interpret it as an unfortunate event carrying an element of evil.

Here, it becomes apparent that the Yorùbá definition of evil aligns with the Western understanding, as it encompasses all that is negative and obstructs humanity's path to happiness. Generally speaking, any experience that causes harm, pain, regret, or impedes the achievement of goals, ideals, happiness, or well-being is categorized as evil.

Ifá says,

> *Ọ̀bẹ́ sínú igbó fẹ̀ṣẹ̀ já gbàwo;*
> *Adífá fún ire, ire ń tìkọ̀lé ọ̀run bọ̀ wá ìkọ̀lé ayé*
> *Ọ̀bẹ́sínú igbó fẹ̀ṣẹ̀ já gbàwo;*
> *Adífá fún ibi, ibi ń tìkọ̀lé ọ̀run bọ̀ wá ìkọ̀lé ayé*
> *Òòjọ́ tí a ríbi ni ibi ń wọlẹ̀,*
> *Òòjọ́ tí a ríre ni ire ń wolé.*

This verse narrates how Ire (Good) and *Ibi* (Bad) were descending from heaven to earth. They were instructed to make the necessary sacrifices. Good complied and made the required sacrifice, while Bad/Evil refused to do so. When Good arrived on earth, it proudly announced its presence, radiating positivity. When Evil arrived, it remained silent and unable to utter a single word. This astonished the people, who sought guidance and consulted Ifá. They swiftly picked Ibi (Evil) and buried it on the same day. Hence the Yorùbá saying, *"ọjọ́ a ríbi ni ibi ń wọlẹ̀."*

Ire is always welcome, permitted to enter and stay, while ibi is not to be entertained or embraced. Every human being is born with a mixture of ibi and ire within them. No matter how cautious, wise, or kind a person is, it is inevitable not to encounter some form of evil in the earthly realm. It may then be crucial for us to reject and repel negative occurrences or influences when they arise, whether obvious or subtle. By doing so, we strive to cultivate an environment and a life filled with goodness and positivity.

The essence of evil lies in causing harm to others. Thus, evil does not necessarily have a religious connotation in Yorùbá culture, and within the Yorùbá context, evil relates more to morality and has little to do with indigenous practices.

The Yorùbá believe evil originates from some spiritual forces other than Òrìṣà. This belief arises from the effects of evil on individuals and its mysterious occurrences. According to the Yorùbá, evil does not stem from a single source but rather from various paranormal forces known as *Ajogun* in Yorùbáland. These forces are scattered throughout the universe. Each force has a specific function and is associated with a particular form of evil. The *Ajogun* importantly includes *Ikú* (Death), *Àrùn* (Disease), *Òfò* (Loss), *Ẹgbà* (Paralysis), *Ọràn* (Trouble), *Èṣe* (Wound/Accident) and *Ìjà* (Fight/Conflict).

Ifá says,

> *Alágbẹ̀dẹ ní fi ibi sínmíní owú kíni*
> *A fibi èyí rìnmìrinmi ẹ̀ tẹlẹ̀*

Adífá fún Ọ̀rúnmìlà,

Níjọ́ tí ikú àti àrùn ń kanlé ẹ yun,

Ajogun gbogbo, wọ́n ń kanlé Ifá ń lílọ

Ifá ní mo fi ikú pin lónìí; métì bá wọn kú mọ́

o

Adìrẹ òpìpì, mo fi ikú pin

Mo ṣe ikú pin lalágbẹ̀dẹ sẹ̀gún-ún.

- Excerpt from Ògúndábèdé

Therefore, it can be inferred that the Yorùbá understanding of evil is multi-dimensional. From the Yorùbá perspective, ibi is an integral part of human existence. This notion is reflected in the saying, "Tibi tire la dá ilé ayé" (the universe was created as a mixture of good and evil). The foundation of this statement can be traced back to our birth. When a child is born, both the placenta and the baby are brought forth by women. The placenta is referred to as "Ìkejì ọmọ" or "olubi ọmọ" in Yorùbá, signifying the baby's second companion. This exemplifies the Yorùbá wisdom that we enter this world together with both good and evil.

> *Bóoru bá mú ìkaàkà làá sùn,*
> *Adífá fún Ọ̀rúnmìlà,*
> *Ifá ó fi ẹgbàá rẹ̀mí nítorí ikú,*
> *Ẹbọ ni wọ́n ní kó ṣe*
> *Ǹjẹ́ bẹ̀mìí ò bá bọ́,*
> *Ajé ń bọ̀*
> *Ọmọ ń bọ̀*
> *Ire gbogbo ń bọ̀ níhìn-ín.*

Translation:

> When it is hot, we sleep face up,
> This is Ifá's message to Ọ̀rúnmìlà,
> Who needed to ransom his own life with two thousands cowries

He was asked to be fully prepared to offer a

sacrifice.

As long as there is life,

There will be money,

There will be children,

There will be good things of life here.

- Excerpt from Èjì Ogbè

CONCEPT OF ẸBỌ IN YORÙBÁ INDÍGENOUS PRACTICES

In Yorùbá, *ẹbọ*, also known as *ètùtù*, means sacrifice or propitiation. Generally, sacrifice is the act of giving up something valued to preserve or achieve other considerations. *Ẹbọ* is a ritual prescribed within *Ifá* or *Òrìṣà* divination, dedicated to a specific being or for a particular purpose. It is a sacrifice made to maintain blessings, ward off evils, seek favour, establish harmony, and restore balance. *Ẹbọ* comprises a combination of symbolic materials or instructions that relate to an individual's specific situation. Its purpose is to bring about a positive, fortunate, or well-balanced outcome. In Yorùbá indigenous practices, once a problem has been identified through divination, it becomes crucial to perform the necessary appeasements.

Many Ifá verses end with this warning:

> *Rírú ẹbọ ní í gbeni,*
>
> *Àìrú ẹbọ kì í gbe ènìyàn,*
>
> *Mọ́ pe wo lékèé,*
>
> *Mọ́ pe Èṣù lólè,*
>
> *Mọ́ wo ọ̀run yànyàn bí ẹni tí kò ní í kú,*
>
> *Mọ́ kọ etí ọ̀gbọin sẹ́bọ.*

Such lines emphasizes rírú ẹbọ (offering sacrifice):

> *Rírú ẹbọ níí gbeni*
>
> *Àìrú ẹbọ kìí gbèèyàn*

Translation:

Sacrificing brings blessings
The neglect of it pays no man.

Ẹbọ can be in form of instruction(s) to follow or resources to offer such as clothing, money, or food. Its primary purpose is to deter negative forces in one's life or path and enhance, catalyse or maintain blessings along one's path. Ẹbọ involves giving up something to attain higher gains and facilitate positive changes in life. It works in conjunction with the elements and forces of the universe. Ẹbọ ensures alignment and harmony with one's destiny, elevates one's prayers, and brings about balanced or positive outcomes. Individuals already in spiritual alignment and in tune with their destinies perform sacrifices to maintain stability. Ẹbọ is an important tool for problem solving after consultation, and every

Odù Ifá speaks about it.

Ifá says,

> *Òfíì, òláà*
>
> *Ìrù eṣin ni kò gbébìkan*
>
> *Adífá fún ire tí í ṣe ọmọ ọlá*
>
> *Ẹbọ ire ni wọn ní kí ọlá ó ṣe*
>
> *Ó gbẹ́bọ ó sì rúbọ*
>
> *Ó gbérù ó sì tù*
>
> *Ẹbọ rẹ̀ fín*
>
> *Ẹbọ rẹ̀ dà*
>
> *Ó ní ẹ wí fún Alárá*
>
> *Ẹ sọ pé mo rí ire*
>
> *Ẹ wí fún Ajerò*
>
> *Ẹ sọ pé mo rí ire*
>
> *Ọ̀ràngún ilé Ìlá, mo rí ire*
>
> *Ire tó ti nù, ire wọlé dé.*

Translation:

Being blown in different directions

The horse tail is not stable

This cast Ifá divination for 'good fortune,' the
child of honour

Honour was instructed to observe the sacrifice
of good fortune

He heard about the sacrifice

And he made the sacrifice

His supplications were accepted

He said they should proclaim it to Alárá,

That he had seen good fortune

Tell it to Ajerò

That I have seen goodness

Ọràngún of Ìláland, I have seen goodness

Goodness that was lost had returned.

-Excerpt from Odù Ifá Ogbè-Alárá

Another Ifá says,

Ojú tí ń pọ́n Awo, àpọ́nkú kọ́

Òṣì tí ń ta Awo, àtalà ni

Bóbá pẹ́ títí a ó fọ̀rọ̀ yìí ṣẹrín-rín

Adífá fún Òrìṣà-Ńlá Ọ̀ṣẹ̀rẹ̀màgbò,

Tí ó fi Arọ ṣe àkọ́rà ẹrú lọ́jà Èjìgbòmẹkùn.

Ẹbọ wọn pe ó ṣe,

Ó gbọ́ rírú ẹbọ, ó rúbọ,

Ó gbérù ó tù kÈṣù

Njẹ, ẹrú tí mo rà ló làmí

Ẹrú tí mo rà ló sọ mí dọba.

Translation:

The suffering of Awo is not eternal

Poverty that is facing Awo will soon turn to prosperity

At the end, Awo will laugh at his/her challenges.

Casted divination for *Òrìṣà-Ńlá Ọ̀ṣẹ̀rẹ̀màgbò,*

Who will buy an handicap as the first slave.

He was instructed to perform sacrifice, he complied

Behold! My slave has brought me wealth

My slave has brought me kingly fortune.

At one time, *Òrìṣà-Ńlá* (also *Ọbàtálá*) faced some challenges. He consulted Ifá, and was advised to perform sacrifices to change his circumstances. He received specific instructions and prescriptions, and he complied. *Òrìṣà-Ńlá Ọṣẹ̀rẹ̀màgbò* journeyed to *Èjìgbòmẹkùn*, faithfully following the prescribed sacrifice and instructions. Who would have believed a disabled person could bring wealth to someone? Yet, the disabled slave brought him wealth.

Ẹbọ has the power to transform adverse situations or redirect the *Ajogun*, forces of misfortune, into blessings and positive outcomes.

Here is an account from *Ọbàrà-Òtùrá*:

> *Ọbàrà túra sílẹ̀, ogun ti lọ*
>
> *Adífá fún Ọrúnmìlà*
>
> *Tí ikú àti àrùn ń kanlé rẹ̀ ẹ́ rè;*
>
> *Ajogun gbogbo ń kanlé Ifá ní lílọ*
>
> *Ẹbọ ni wọ́n ní kí baba ó mú ṣe*
>
> *Ó gbẹ́bọ, ó rúbọ*
>
> *Kò pẹ́ kò jìnnà,*
>
> *Ẹ wá bá ni lárùṣẹ́ ogun*

Translation:

> *Ọbàrà* relax, the war is over
>
> This is Ifá's message for *Ọrúnmìlà,*
>
> When death and affliction were heading for his home
>
> And all destructive forces were trooping into his house
>
> He was advised to make sacrifice, he complied

Not too long or far, before we join to celebrate

victory.   31

These references emphasize that performing

sacrifice is beneficial, and lack thereof is chaotic.

MYTHS aBOUT Ē$Ū

The Yorùbá people firmly believe that nothing in the world occurs by chance; rather, everything in this vast universe is brought into existence by *Olódùmarè*. In this intricate belief system, it is understood that both visible and invisible entities within the universe are creations of *Olódùmarè*. *Èṣù*, too, falls into this category of created beings, existing since the primordial times.

As the source of life in both the seen and unseen realms of the universe, *Olódùmarè* is regarded as the origin of *Èṣù* and other *Irúnmọlẹ̀*. Therefore, the Yorùbá firmly believe that Èṣù's existence can be traced back to Olódùmarè.

Èṣù holds a significant position among the Òrìṣà in Yorùbá theology. He is considered one of the primordial and original divine beings in Yorùbá pantheon, alongside other notable figures such as Ọrúnmìlà, the deity of wisdom; Ògún, who governs iron, war and technically the minister of justice; and Ọbàtálá, the creative divinity and eldest among the Yorùbá divinities. Olódùmarè is the ultimate origin and source of all beings, including the divinities themselves. In fact, many verses of *Ifá* ends with the saying that a certain person was praising his *Awo* (priest), the Awo was praising *Ifá*, but *Ifá* was also praising *Olódùmarè;* it is only Olódùmarè, who has no one to praise.

Here is an excerpt from *Ogbèyẹ̀kú:*

Ó ń yin Babaláwo;

Babaláwo ń yin Ifá;

Ifá ń yin Olódùmarè,

Olódùmarè nìkan ni kò lẹ́ni tí yóò f'ìyìn fún.

Translation:

He was praising the Ifá priest;

The priest was praising Ifá;

Ifá was praising Olódùmarè, (the Supreme Being)

It is only Olódùmarè, who has no one to praise.

Èṣù and other Irúnmọlẹ̀ were messengers of Olódùmarè on earth. They came to deliver the mandate given to them by Olódùmarè. According to a narrative from Ifá, Èṣù is depicted as a tall man. In his praise, it is mentioned that he walks majestically through the groundnut plantation—*Ń lọ nínú ẹ̀pà, ìpàkọ́ ẹ̀ẹ̀ fé, opẹ́lọpẹ́ gíga tí baba ga.*

In linguistic sense, the word Èṣù is formed by combining 'È' meaning 'you' with 'ṣù' meaning 'to harmonize or bring together.' Thus, Èṣù can be understood as "the one who brings together (or guides) for the purpose of harmonious co-existence."

This breakdown of Èṣù can be further simplified by considering it as a combination of 'È' (meaning 'act of') and 'ṣù' (meaning 'harmonize or bring together'). Therefore, Èṣù can be viewed as the Irúnmọlẹ̀ who promotes harmony and unifies people and things.

NaTURe anD ROLe OF ÈṢÙ

Èṣù is a prominent and complex *Irúnmọlẹ̀* (deity) with many indispensable roles. He is a force of balance, within the indigenous Yorùbá religion charged with responsibility of carrying or noting the peoples' sacrifices and delivering them to the right office. He holds a special position as the liaison officer between humans, other divinities and Olódùmarè. Èṣù acts as a mediator between *Ikole Ọrun* (heaven) and *Ayé* (earth), thereby serving as a confidential secretary. He is a messenger, closest to heaven among the Irúnmọlẹ̀ that descended from heaven to earth.

Èṣù exists as the inspector general or the universal police. He leads the charge in dispensing information, similar to the role of a central intelligence agency. He can be likened to a skilled investigator who uncovers and holds accountable those who commit wrongdoings. These are fundamental responsibilities assigned to him by Olódùmarè, and thereby grants Èṣù a distinctive role and influence in the Yorùbá pantheon.

Èṣù, also known as the *Onílé Oríta,* the possessor of crossroads—an emblematic position of spiritual significance, possesses both malevolent and benevolent aspects, implying that he is not inherently evil but rather a neutral entity existing between the realms of good and bad; yes or no;

right or left; wrong or right, etc. Therefore, it is crucial to recognize that the perception of police officers as benevolent or malevolent, depends on the context in which they operate. Just as the moon reveals only a fraction of its luminescence during a lunar eclipse; the multifaceted nature of their role remains obscured without a comprehensive understanding of the circumstances.

Èṣù sees across heaven and earth, and know whatever is about to happen to a man, whether good or bad. He has the capacity to alter circumstances or work in favour of individuals based on the consideration bestowed upon him - *ẹni tó rúbọ lÈṣù ń gbè.*

According to the Yorùbá proverb, *"Bí òní ṣe rí, òla kò rí bẹ́ẹ̀ ló mú Babaláwo dífá ọrọọrún."* Every day is different, there is no day that is the same; this is the reason a Babaláwo casts Ifá divination every five days. In Yorùbá Indigenous order, if someone experiences a troubling dream or encounters an unusual sign, they may consult Ifá to determine the underlying issue. Through this process, they can discern whether the sign or dream is a blessing or something else entirely. Such consultation would offer guidance on how to counteract the impending evil or secure the promised blessing. When one diligently follows the directives provided, Èṣù ensures that the intended recipient receives the blessing without hindrance. If it is a negative or evil message, Èṣù would also ensure to avert it — *"Ikú kì í jẹun ẹni, kó tún pani; àrùn kì í jẹun ẹni kó gbéni dè."* (Death or sickness does not feast on someone after eating one's food). Èṣù plays a vital role in averting evil or directing goodness and blessings towards any individual who maintains a good stand.

There is a collection of stories attributed to Èṣù in sacred texts.

An Ifá says,

> *Ìwọ Ìwòrì, Èmi Ìwòrì*
>
> *Ìwòrì di méjì ó dẹrín*
>
> *Adífá fún Ọlọfin*
>
> *Tí wọn ní kó rúbọ àìkú*
>
> *Kò pe Awo léké, kò pe Èṣù lólè*
>
> *Ó gbọ rírú ẹbọ, ó rú u;*
>
> *Kò kú mọ, ikú yẹ lórí rẹ*
>
> *Ó wá ń yin àwọn Awo rẹ*
>
> *Àwọn Awo rẹ ń yin Ifá*
>
> *Ifá ń yin Olódùmarè,*
>
> *Olódùmarè nìkan ni ò lẹni àáfiyìn fún.*
>
> *Ẹṣẹ tó nà, ijó fáá*
>
> *Orin ló kó síi lẹnu.*

Translation:

You are Ìwòrì, I am *Ìwòrì*

Two Ìwòrì is a blessing

This is Ifá's message to *Ọlọfin* during his tribulation

He was asked to make sacrifice for longevity

He did not call his Ifá Priest a liar neither Èṣù a thief;

He complied, and so escaped death

He thanked his Ifá Priest, who in turn thanked Ifá

He burst out dancing and singing the praise of Olódùmarè through Ifá.

Here is another Ifá account:

Àgádágodo-gbà, the Awo of Alákìsà

Casted Ifá divination for Alákìsà,

The one who was doing everything

But neither give Ifá nor Èṣù to eat

Yet the sacrifice to Èṣù is very important

Let us offer the prescribed sacrifice to Èṣù,

So that he can have it to our account...

\- Excerpt from Ọ̀wọ́rínṣogbè

For instance, if evil looms over someone, Èṣù, with his ability to perceive events across heaven and earth, becomes aware but he can do nothing unless the intended victim take proper actions. Through consultation with Ifá, one can gain insight into the impending danger and receive instructions on the necessary sacrifice to avert such a calamity. When the person follows the prescribed ritual and presents the offering, Èṣù then becomes involved because he must attend to every sacrifice accordingly. As evil or any Ajogun (negative force) approaches, they must pass through Èṣù since he is the gatekeeper and intermediary between malevolent (or destructive) spirits known as Ajogun and the Irúnmọlẹ̀, as well as the human beings. Èṣù would take from the sacrifice made by the person and offer it to the approaching Ajogun.

On the other hand, when blessings or goodness are destined to arrive, Èṣù ensures that they reach the intended recipient. When such person has prepared offerings like Ọ́gẹ̀dẹ̀ (Banana), Ẹyẹlé (Pigeon), and others, Èṣù guides these blessings to the quarters of the individual who made the sacrifices.

For emphasis, Èṣù assumes multiple roles—of gatekeeper, central intelligence officer, relation officer, messenger, carrier, and chief law enforcer, among others—as assigned to him by *Olódùmarè*. In that sphere of obligations, he occupies a significant position in Yorùbá spirituality, facilitating the flow of blessings and safeguarding individuals from harm as directed by Olódùmarè. Èṣù perpetually occupies the middle ground between opposing forces, regulating the realms of happiness, joy, destruction, hopelessness, and sorrow. He teaches that every issue has multiple perspectives. He is credited with remarkable accomplishments, such as establishing balance and creating paths. He is indispensable for maintaining order in life's intricate web.

Èṣù safeguards towns, villages, priests, priestesses, devotees, and anyone who brings presents to him from evil machinations.

Èṣù has the ability to disrupt or spoil things if they are not carried out according to prescribed procedures. As the enforcer of Olódùmarè's will among divinities and humans, Èṣù can bring both good and bad outcomes to individuals based on their alignment with Olódùmarè's desires. This is far from concept of being a "devil." Èṣù embodies both good and evil, representing the coexistence of positive and negative forces in the world, acknowledging their presence and influence.

Èṣù embodies a two-sided nature that permeates every aspect of existence. His adeptness in fulfilling his duties and responsibilities knows no bounds, often employing extraordinary and unconventional methods.

Hence, he is praised as the *Onílé Oríta,* the one always at the middle of divergent world forces.

Abẹ́lẹ́kún sunkún kẹ́rù ó bẹlẹ́kún,
the one who cries in a more terrible way than the bereaved/afflicted.

Ẹlẹ́kún ń sunmi, láaróyè ń sẹ̀jẹ̀,
the concerned shed tears, but Èṣù shed blood.

Abónímín sumí, kẹ̀rù ó ba onímín,
the one who passed stool more than the
affected.

Onímín ń sumí, láaróyè ń ṣù fun,
the affected passed stool but Èṣù almost
passed his lungs.

Èṣù becomes deeply concerned whenever he is
called upon to intervene in a matter. He shows
great concern for those who are deprived or in
need. Èṣù is a compassionate entity who genuinely
cares about every situation he is invited into.

Èṣù, during his lifetime, shared a close bond with
Ọrúnmìlà Bara-Àgbọnnìrègún, the custodian of
Ifá. According to Ifá oral literature, Èṣù originally

resided in *Ilé-Ifẹ̀* but gained a large following when he moved to *Orílé-Kétu* (in the now Benin Republic), where he enjoyed fame.

YORÙBÁ INDIGENOUS RELIGION AND Ẹ̀ṢÙ WORSHIP

Worship, like in other religions, is an integral part of Yorùbá spirituality. It serves as a means for individuals to express their reverence towards the Supreme Being and other spiritual entities. It involves communication and communion between humans and the spiritual realm, facilitating the maintenance and restoration of the divine-human relationship. Worship is the outward manifestation of spiritual realities through physical acts, serving as a medium through which divine power is made accessible to humans. As the Yorùbá are inherently religious people, worship permeates every aspect of our lives, from beginning to end. Thus, the Yorùbá Indigenous Religion refers to the native faith of the Yorùbá people, passed down through various means, including art, oral traditions/literatures, crafts, proverbs, stories, songs, folklore, and wise sayings.

Yorùbá Indigenous Religion is how the Yorùbá traditionally connect with the spiritual or enter a relationship with the divine. The awareness of the presence of deities is constant among Yorùbá people, regardless of our location or activities, and our worship occurs on a regular or occasional intervals. For instance, when ancestral shrines (*Ojúbọ or Òkè-Ìpọrí*, for the initiated) are present in people's homes, daily worship occurs.

Worship can be both private and public, following a liturgical process similar to other religions practiced worldwide.

The worship of Èṣù is widespread throughout Yorùbáland. This is evidenced by the fact that every household must have an Èṣù altar called *Ojúbọ Èṣù or Èṣù Ode,* situated outside the compound. This signifies that Èṣù's shrine or altar is typically located outside compounds, towns, or villages because of his impartial nature. The shrine is often represented by a stone slab, a slanted piece of rough laterite embedded in the ground, or it may take the form of a mud or wooden effigy. The worship of Èṣù, like other deities in Yorùbá culture, is ritualistic and adheres to a prescribed order that must be followed meticulously.

The elements involved in Èṣù's worship include *Owó Ẹyọ* (cowries), *Àkùkọ Adìẹ* (roosters), *Òbúkọ* (he-goats), *Agbo* (rams), *Obì* (kola nuts), *Orógbó* (bitter kola), *Ìgbín* (snails), *Ẹ̀kọ* (cooked pap), *Epo Pupa* (Palm oil), and more.

Èṣù has followers and devotees around called the Òmìsìn of Èṣù. They name their children according to their experience, and devotion to Èṣù. Yorùbá names encapsulate the circumstances of birth, the richness of culture and history, and the interconnectedness of family. They are vessels of significance, conveying essential truths and relevant facts that define the individuals who bear them. There is Èṣùlékè, Èṣùbìyí, Èṣùdárà, Èṣùyẹmí, Èṣùwándé, and many more. If Èṣù was an evil character, there would be no such naming because the Yorùbá give names referencing whatever is precious to their world.

Unfortunately, *"Èṣù mọ́ ṣe mí"* (Èṣù, do not implicate me) is an expression often misunderstood, with its essence and deeper meaning overlooked. It does not imply that Èṣù is an entity filled with evil for us, our friends, or relatives. It merely signifies the innate human desire to avoid every form of harm. After all, nobody wishes or prays for any harm to befall them; not even from *Olódùmarè,* the Supreme Being.

Nonetheless, it is natural for anyone to feel anger when they are offended, including Olódùmarè. Similarly, if one offends Èṣù, Ọrúnmìlà, Ògún, Ṣàngó, Ọya or any other Òrìṣà, they may become angry and respond accordingly. This applies to every human being as well. So, when we say, *"Èṣù mọ́ ṣe mí"* (Èṣù, do not implicate me), *"Ṣàngó mọ́ ṣe mí,"* or *"Ògún mọ́ ṣe mí,"* it is a prayer for well-being just like how we would not wish that Olódùmarè implicates us. It is a plea for guidance and protection in our lives.

Èṣù has a profound vision and sees through the happenings of both heaven and earth. He knows before the arrival of good or the emergence of evil. He possesses the power to guide and channel forthcoming goodness towards individuals. Likewise, he has the power to thwart evil, but only if the individual targeted by the *Ajogun* (misfortune or evil) has adhered to proper conduct and performed necessary sacrifice.

Àfi ṣóńṣó abẹ,
Adífá fún Èṣù Ọdàrà tí wọn dẹrù burúkú lé lórí
Èṣù Ọdàrà ò lórí à ń gbẹrù lé, à fi ṣóńṣó abẹ.

Relationship Between Ọrúnmìlà and Èṣù

Ifá corpus contains numerous accounts and references to Èṣù, primarily due to the close relationship between Èṣù and Ọrúnmìlà. While Èṣù interacts with other Irúnmọlẹ̀ (divinities), it is Ọrúnmìlà who possesses the deepest understanding of Èṣù. Whenever Ọrúnmìlà prepares a sacrifice, it is Èṣù who carries it to heaven.

Ifá says,

> *Kárójú-ẹni-ká-sọ-dáadáa,*
>
> *Kápẹ̀yìndà-tán-ká-sọ-bá-mîí.*
>
> *Èyí tá a bá tètè wí lọlọ́run gbà á gbọ́*
>
> *Adífá fún Ọ̀rúnmìlà, Ifá ń lọ rèé sọrẹ́ Ọ̀dàrà nífẹ̀*
>
> *Ire Ajé tí mo wí àná ńkọ́?*
>
> *Ọ̀dàrà, darí ire tèmi sí mi, Ọ̀dàrà*
>
> *Ire aya, ire ọmọ, ire gbogbo tí mo wí àná ńkọ́?*
>
> *Ọ̀dàrà, darí ire tèmi sí mi, Ọ̀dàrà.*

- Excerpt from *Ìdin-Amìnlẹ̀kẹ̀*

Ọ̀rúnmìlà faced numerous challenges on earth, including the absence of a wife (at a time), children, wealth, and other blessings. Feeling the weight of his struggles, Ọ̀rúnmìlà sought the assistance of *Kárójú-ẹni-ká-sọ-dáadáa* and *Kápẹ̀yìndà-tán-kásọ bá mîi,* his diviners who possessed deep knowledge. They casted Ifá divination, and *Ìdin-Amìnlẹ̀kẹ̀* corpus appeared. The Ifá corpus revealed a specific sacrifice that Ọrúnmìlà needed to make to address his problems. The diviners instructed him to deliver the sacrifice and message to Èṣù.

Following the prescribed instructions, Ọrúnmìlà meticulously prepared the necessary offerings and presented them to Èṣù. *Ẹbọ* (sacrifice), as mentioned earlier, is not only an appeasement but also a form of *Àrokò,* with its coded message. As Èṣù beheld the sacrifice, he intuitively comprehended the meaning behind each ingredient employed. Èṣù then embarked on a journey to heaven, where he summoned every desirable blessing to come to Ọrúnmìlà's aid.

Ọrúnmìlà was filled with curiosity that he considered repeating the same sacrifice. He began praising his Awo (priests), yet the Awo reciprocated by praising Ifá, and in turn, Ifá praised Olódùmarè (Supreme Being).

Here is another account from Ifá corpus:

Àríwoníyangí

Àgbàlagbà emèèṣà, àpa-à-délé ò jẹ́ á mọ
pé Ológbò ń sọdẹ,

Adífá fún Ọrúnmìlà, Ifá ó rán Èṣù Ọdàrà
níṣẹ́ ọlà lọ́run

Èṣù wá jàdí tán ó jẹ Ẹlẹ́dẹ̀;

Gọrọrọ, Èṣù mọ̀ ń bì

Èṣù bì títí baba mọ Ajé;

Gọrọrọ, Èṣù mọ̀ ń bì

Èṣù bì èjìgbàrà ìlẹ̀kẹ̀ baba mokùn;

Gọrọrọ, Èṣù mọ̀ ń bì

Èṣù wá jọkọ́ tán, ó jẹ Ẹlẹ́dẹ̀

Gọrọrọ, Èṣù mọ̀ ń bì.

Here, Ọrúnmìlà sent Èṣù a message of wealth to heaven. This is because all goodness comes from heaven to earth and Èṣù is the messenger for every Irúnmọlẹ̀. He is sent on errand wherever necessary. In this particular instance, when Èṣù got to heaven, on Ọrúnmìlà's errand, there was no way he could carry every goodness at once. With his power, however, he swallowed (and stored) each of these blessings which he then vomited upon reaching Ọrúnmìlà back on earth.

While some believe this, that Èṣù serves as the right-hand divinity to Ọrúnmìlà, running errands on his behalf, others suggest that Èṣù taught Ọrúnmìlà the very art of divination. In actual sense according to Ifá, Èṣù is not a subordinate character among the divinities, but he plays a crucial role in their interactions. Although there is a cooperative relationship between all the Irúnmọlẹ̀, Èṣù and Ọrúnmìlà are especially close, and it is evident that Èṣù holds a significant connection to Ọrúnmìlà.

Ifá says,

> *Ká dijú ká ṣe bí ẹni kú;*
> *Káwo ẹni tí ó sèdárò ẹni*
> *Kárìn gbẹ̀rẹ̀ ká fẹṣẹ̀ kọ pàrà;*
> *Ká wo ẹni tí ṣeni pẹ̀lẹ́*
> *Adífá fún Ọrúnmìlà,*
> *Baba ń fi ikú tan gbogbo Irúnmọlẹ̀*
> *Ǹjẹ́ Ọrúnmìlà ò kú, baba wà lájà;*
> *Ẹkún ara wọn ni wọ́n ń sun.*

Translation:

Close your eyes and feign death,

See who will mourn you;

Run and make sure you trip,

Observe those who'll be sympathetic.

Casted divination for Ọ̀rúnmìlà

Who feigned death to test the Irúnmọlẹ̀

Ọ̀rúnmìlà is not dead, he hid in the attic

They were mourning for themselves, not me.

- Excerpt from *Odù Ifá Èjì Ogbè*

This Ifá narrative recounts a story that reveals Ọ̀rúnmìlà's curiosity about who loves and cares for him the most among the Irúnmọlẹ̀. To test them, Ọ̀rúnmìlà devised a plan. He wrapped a banana stem with white cloth and hid in the attic. In the middle of the night, Ọ̀rúnmìlà's children began to cry, announcing their father's supposed demise. When Ṣàngó heard the news, he grew furious, as he had properties entrusted to Ọ̀rúnmìlà. Ṣàngó approached Ọ̀rúnmìlà's children to claim what was rightfully his. Similarly, Ògún, Eégún, and the other Irúnmọlẹ̀ reacted in comparable ways to Ṣàngó.

Èṣù Ọ̀dàrà, while getting his hair trimmed, received word of Ọrúnmìlà's passing. Although the barber had only cut half of his hair, Èṣù could not wait. He stood up abruptly, leaving one side of his head barbed and the other side with hair. This led to the eulogy: *"Ọ̀fárí apá kan dá apá kan sí"* (The one who had one side barbed, and one side with hair). Since that day, Èṣù has left a portion of his hair uncut. While others shed tears, blood trickled from Èṣù's eyes, surprising those around him. They inquired about what Ọrúnmìlà owed Èṣù. Èṣù replied that what Ọrúnmìlà owed him was insignificant compared to his life. Despite receiving consolation, Èṣù continued to weep. While others departed for their homes, Èṣù remained, unable to believe that Ọrúnmìlà had truly passed away.

After some time, Ọrúnmìlà emerged from the attic, revealing that the cries were directed towards themselves. He declared, "Ọrúnmìlà is not dead but in the attic." This incident deeply moved Ọrúnmìlà because it demonstrated Èṣù's profound love and care. As a result, Ọrúnmìlà made a vow that whenever he wished to eat anything, he would first offer a part of it to Èṣù. Ọrúnmìlà offers priority to Èṣù because he loved him more at his staged funeral. Furthermore, his children and followers were required to present their offerings to Èṣù before partaking in any meal.

Consequently, the *Babaláwo* (Ifá priests) traditionally possess an in-depth understanding of Èṣù's nature and role because of the close relationship between Èṣù and Ọrúnmìlà during their lifetime. Their roles complement each other,

with Èṣù and Ọ̀rúnmìlà always near each other—
wherever you see Ọ̀rúnmìlà, Èṣù is nearby.

Although, Ọ̀rúnmìlà bears the responsibility of
receiving divine messages from Olódùmarè
through divination and declaring His will to
the world; it is imperative to adhere to Èṣù's
declarations, as he is mandated to enforce
Olódumarè's will. Ọ̀rúnmìlà, recognizing the
importance of Èṣù's functions, consistently
honours him by offering Èṣù priority in meals
and drinks, alongside specific appeasements
for particular tasks. Thus, every Babaláwo must
have a representation of Èṣù in their compound,
where they offer and present such rituals. Equally,
the Babaláwo maintain the strong connection
between Èṣù and Ọ̀rúnmìlà till today.

MANIFESTATIONS AND CATEGORIES OF ÈṢÙ

ifferent categories arise based on a specific work or message assigned to a particular manifestation of Èṣù. It is important to note that these categories do not imply the existence of multiple Èṣù entities; rather, they indicate the location of the shrine, form of the representation and nature of the assigned task or message. The name of each *Èṣù* may also be influenced by the type of worship or offerings presented at the shrine and manifestation. The *Òmìsìn Èṣù* are the followers or devotees of Èṣù while the *Àwòrò Èṣù* are those initiated into Èṣù – they are the ones who serve as Èṣù priests or priestesses.

We have the following manifestations and sacred representation of Èṣù:

1. *Èṣù Ìlú:* This is a representation or icon of Èṣù that is primarily installed for a town or settlement. Traditionally, Èṣù is associated with junctions. This representation is found at a junction (Oríta) or at the far end or border of the town. Its purpose is to guide and protect the town. Any form of sacrifice or offering made for the town is usually presented before this Èṣù.

2. *Èṣù Òde:* This is an expression of Èṣù that is typically installed in front of a building or

house. It is made for protection and to present offerings, thereby serving other household use or need for Èṣù. It could be a small mound of earth in front of a house, palace, farmstead, and other locations. In ancient times, it was rare to find a house without Èṣù, whether the occupants were devotees or not. For example:

- *Èṣù Ààfin,* as the name suggests is a manifestation typically situated in front of king's palace, ensuring protection and maintaining peace within the royal domain. It is customary for all Yorùbá kings to have this icon of Èṣù in their palaces, as they desire harmony and tranquility within their realm.

- *Èṣù Oko* is a manifestation at farmstead, and it serves several purposes and need of Èṣù on farmland. It safeguards crops from theft, protecting the farmers' harvest, and it is believed to bring about abundant yields and a bountiful harvest.

3. *Èṣù Àwúre:* Ògèdè (banana), Epo Pupa (palm oil) and others are commonly presented before this manifestation of Èṣù, specially installed for blessing and invocation. The carved image or wooden representation of this manifestation of Èṣù would have an elongated backward occipital lobe called Ògọ. Another form of this Èṣù Àwúre can be made with fly whisks attached to cowrie shells (Owó Ẹyọ).

4. *Èṣù Agbẹbọ-Yárun:* This form of Èṣù, dedicated for ẹbọ, carries the sacrifices from earth to heaven. It is commonly associated and popular with the Babaláwo (Ifá Priest). After every sacrifice or ritual is performed, it is placed before this Èṣù. It is a must have for every Babaláwo to have in their compound.

5. *Èṣù Ìrànṣẹ:* This form of Èṣù is usually sent on errand to apprehend an offender. The

prescribed ritual for this Èṣù will bring troubles or problems upon the offender or criminal for whom it is invoked. What distinguishes it, is its sensitivity to specific elements of worship or sacrificial offerings that can enrage and cause havoc when directed toward a target/criminal. If someone seeks to punish an offender, they would take offerings (like *Àdí,* palm kernel oil and other substance Èṣù despises) before its shrine, mention the offender's name, express their displeasure, and invoke Èṣù to arise and fight or defend them.

We have other manifestations, like *Èṣù Ìṣọ́lẹ́, Èṣù Ọjà,* and others. In a sense, Èṣù Ọjà belongs to the category of Èṣù Ìlú since it is a shrine situated in marketplaces to protect against evil influences and ensure the well-being of both buyers and sellers. It is believed to bring about prosperous sales for the merchants. In some cases, the shrines are constructed with walls and roofs, while in other instances, they may appear unremarkable, blending in with the surrounding environment. Example of *Èṣù Ọjà* is *Èṣù Akẹsán in Ọ̀yọ́-Aláàfin*.

The main difference between those expressions or manifestations of Èṣù is the role or purpose specially assigned to each installation. Although *yangí* (mound of earth) is used for most installations, whether Èṣù Ìlú or Èṣù Ọjà, the mixture of ingredients and the recited incantations slightly differ. And such is the role or message that each delivers.

Note: There is an *Ìbọ* or *Ògọ Èṣù* that is considered the *Ìpọ̀rí Èṣù*, the primary or main icon of Èṣù. It is usually found with Èṣù devotees *(Àwòrò Èṣù)*. This representation serves general purposes. It can be invoked for childbirth, protection, blessings, and all other roles of Èṣù on earth.

WORLD OF SATAN/DEVIL

Among the multitude of world religions, Christianity and Islam share remarkable similarities in their understanding of the universe, viewing it as the creation of God. In the Judeo-Christian sacred text, known as the Bible, this Supreme Being is referred to as God (Yahweh); while in Islam's sacred book, the Qur'an, he is known as Allah. Both religions firmly believe that God is the Creator of everything in the vast expanse of the universe. Furthermore, they concur that an entity exists in constant opposition to God, commonly referred to as Satan or Devil in both sacred texts. While God/Allah is universally perceived as omnipotent, embodying goodness, mercy, and omniscience; the Satan/Devil, in stark contrast, is characterized by attributes that stand in direct opposition to those of God.

The term "Satan" originates from the Hebrew word meaning "adversary" or "accuser." The Bible is divided into two sections, Old Testament (also known as the Hebrew Bible) and New Testament. In the Hebrew Bible, Satan was not a proper name but rather referred to an adversary or opponent. In early Jewish traditions, there was no concept of a devil, demons, or hell. Instead, evil and suffering were attributed to God Himself. The book of Isaiah even states that God creates both light and darkness, peace and woe.

In the Hebrew Bible, the term "Satan" is used in different contexts. It is applied to human adversaries. It is also used to describe celestial beings, often referred to as angelic beings or "sons of God." These celestial adversaries, seen in stories like Balaam and the Angel, served as loyal servants of God, fulfilling specific roles assigned to them.

The book of Job presents the most significant portrayal of Satan as an adversary in the Hebrew Bible. Satan challenges God to test Job's loyalty by inflicting suffering upon him. Even in this story, Satan is not considered genuinely evil. He is probably a member of God's court, tasked with observing and reporting the behaviour of God's people.

HISTORY AND ORIGIN OF SATAN

n Judeo-Christian tradition, the term "Satan" from its early usage, as mentioned above, is a general term meaning "adversary" or "accuser" but evolved to its later association with a celestial figure who opposes God and embodies evil. The concept of Satan as a fallen angel and the embodiment of all evil and suffering in the world became more prominent in the Persian period influenced by Zoroastrianism, a religion that introduced the idea of dualism, with a separate evil being opposing the good God.

In the Old Testament, the term "Satan" is initially used to describe human adversaries or stumbling blocks. It is later applied to celestial servants of God, such as the angel in the story of Balaam (Numbers 22:22), the accuser in the Book of Job (Job 2:1-6), and the accuser in the vision of Joshua (Zechariah 3:1-2). These instances present Satan as a "seemingly" loyal servant of God, carrying out specific roles like observing human behaviour and challenging individuals in a legal or moral sense.

As time progressed, the concept of Satan expanded and developed. In the Book of 1 Chronicles, Satan is mentioned as the one who incites David to take a census, signifying a more active role in influencing human actions. The Life of Adam and Eve (in the book of Genesis) introduces the association of Satan with the serpent in the Garden of Eden, which became a common assumption in later interpretations of the Scriptures. Other Jewish texts, such as 1 Enoch and the Book of Jubilees, further elaborated on the fall of angelic beings who corrupted humanity and brought suffering into the world.

However, the New Testament solidified Satan's role as the most powerful opponent of God, Jesus Christ, and humanity. Whether one believes in the reality of Satan or considers him a product of centuries of speculation and theological interpretation is a matter of personal belief and religious interpretation. Satan's presence is seen as influential and pervasive in the world, representing the embodiment of evil according to Christian tradition. Although the history and origin of Satan is complex, different interpretations and beliefs about Satan exist among different religious denominations and individuals. An attempt to dig out the origin and evolution of the word "Satan" is not the essence of this book, but to give a background knowledge and general belief about Satan.

Nature of Satan

Numerous revered figures like Abraham, Moses, King David, the Virgin Mary, Prophet Muhammad and Jesus of Nazareth have played significant roles in shaping Abrahamic religions, but none have held as much infamy and fear-inducing power as Satan, the fallen angel in Christianity and a supernatural creature made of smokeless fire in Islam. Satan is portrayed as the enemy of God, ruler of hell, and the source of evil and suffering.

While the Old Testament of the Bible does not present Satan as the embodiment of evil, subsequent texts contribute to the development of Satan as a powerful adversary in Christianity and its later characterization as a distinct figure can be traced back to various influences.

BELIEF ABOUT SATAN ACCORDING TO BIBLE

2 Enoch 29:1-4, presents a widely recognized tale about the origins of Satan and his fall from grace while drawing inspiration from earlier scriptures, particularly Isaiah 14:12 and Ezekiel 28:17-18. In this account, Satan is portrayed as a prominent figure in the celestial army known as the "sabaoth" or angelic hosts. Together with his followers, he attempts to overthrow the Kingdom of God, driven by his desire for personal power. Unfortunately for Satan, his rebellion fails, leading

to his expulsion from heaven. He is described falling endlessly into a place referred to as the "bottomless pit."

Satan is regarded a spiritual being, a creature mentioned in Ezekiel 28:13-18. It is stated that he once resided in the gardens of Eden (as the author of Revelation describes Satan as "the ancient serpent" in Revelation 12:9; 20:2), adorned with precious stones as his covering. The passage describes his beauty, with carnelian, topaz, jasper, chrysolite, beryl, onyx, sapphire, carbuncle, and emerald adorning him. He possessed settings and engravings of gold. He was appointed as an anointed guardian cherub and dwelled on the holy mountain of God, amidst fiery stones. He walked blamelessly until wickedness was found in him (Ezekiel 28:13-18).

Satan is an opponent of Jesus who attempted to deceive him (Mark 1:13). He is prince of the devils and opposing force to God (Luke 11:15-19; Matthew 12:24-27; Mark 3:22-23:26). He is equally a rebel angel, a spirit creature who opposes God. The Bible calls Satan "the ruler of this world." (John 12:31). He uses "lying signs" and "deception" to accomplish his aims.

According to Bible, Jesus' ministry puts a temporary end to Satan's reign (Luke 10:18) and the conversion of the gentiles leads them from Satan to God (Acts 26:18). Although Satan endangers the Christian communities, he will fall in Christ's final act of salvation, as described in the book of Revelation.

BeLieF aBOUT SaTan ACCORDiNG TO QUR'an

In Islam, Satan, known as *Iblis*, originated from the story of Adam and Eve (in the Qur'an). According to Islamic belief, *Iblis* was a *jinn* (a supernatural creature made of smokeless fire) who was created before humans. It is said that when God commanded the angels and *jinn* to prostrate before Adam (Qur'an 18:50), *Iblis* refused, out of pride and arrogance. As a result, he was casted out of God's favour and became Satan, vowing to lead humanity astray. In Islamic theology, Satan is seen as a tempter who tries to divert humans from the path of righteousness and obedience to God.

Jinn are mentioned in the Qur'an and are believed to inhabit a parallel realm alongside humans. Jinn possess free will, just like humans, and can be either good or evil. They have powers beyond human capabilities, such as invisibility, shape-shifting, and the ability to possess individuals. Jinn are believed to live in various places, including deserts, ruins, and unclean areas. While some jinn are seen as mischievous or malevolent, others may be benevolent and follow a path of faith. Islamic teachings emphasize seeking God's protection from the influence of evil jinn.

In Islam, Satan, also known as Iblis, is portrayed as a rebellious and deceitful creature (Qur'an 7:27; 20:120,121; 36:60). His primary works and nature, as described in the Quran, includes:

1. Temptation and Misguidance: Satan's main objective is to lead humans astray from the path of righteousness and obedience to God. He tempts individuals to commit sins and encourages disbelief or disobedience.

Quranic Reference: "Indeed, Satan is an enemy to you; so take him as an enemy. He only invites his party to be among the companions of the Blaze." (Quran 35:6)

2. Whispering and Inciting Evil: Satan whispers evil suggestions and thoughts into the hearts of humans, trying to influence their actions and lead them away from God's guidance.

Quranic Reference: "Satan threatens you with poverty and orders you to immorality while Allah promises you forgiveness from Him and bounty. And Allah is all-encompassing and knowing." (Quran 2:268)

3. False Promises and Deception: Satan employs deception to make sin appear enticing and promises worldly pleasures and success, leading people to make choices that are harmful to their spiritual well-being (Qur'an 2:36).

Quranic Reference: "Satan promises them and arouses desire in them. But Satan does not promise them except delusion." (Quran 4:120)

4. Enmity towards Humanity: Satan harbors deep enmity towards humans due to their creation and has made it his mission to lead them away from the path of righteousness (Qur'an 15:32-43).

Quranic Reference: "Indeed, Satan is an enemy to you; so take him as an enemy. He only invites his party to be among the companions of the Blaze." (Quran 35:6)

The Qur'an warns believers to be vigilant and seek refuge in God from the influence and temptations of Satan. It emphasizes the importance of faith, righteous deeds, and seeking God's guidance as a means to resist Satan's deceptions.

OUR WORLD WITHOUT SATAN

t is crucial to note that the Yorùbá's concept and worldview, in contrast to Christianity and Islam, does not present a structural opposition between God and the Devil. The Yorùbá understanding of Èṣù does not align with the Christian's Devil or Islamic's Shaytan, as Èṣù does not stand in opposition to the work of God. In Christianity (especially New Testament), the Devil is seen as an adversary to God's plan of salvation for humanity. He tempts people and leads them astray from the righteous path. This incorrect identification of Èṣù with the Devil was further reinforced by the translation of the Bible into the Yorùbá language. Consequently, Èṣù came to be regarded as synonymous with the Devil (and Satan). As a result, a misconception of Èṣù emerged within the Yorùbá Christian community. Islam also adopted a similar perspective, viewing Èṣù through the lens of Shaytan. The misinterpretation resulting from scriptural translations, where Yorùbá Muslims also equated Èṣù with Shaytan contributed to the Yorùbá Islamic misconception of Èṣù.

Èṣù holds a significant position as one of the *Irúnmọlẹ̀*, an entity representing balance and rationality. He has never rebelled against *Olódùmarè,* the Supreme Being, nor has he ever attempted to assume Olódùmarè's role. Èṣù has never been expelled from the heaven (*Ìkọ̀lé ọ̀run)*, but he continues to maintain a harmonious relationship with Olódùmarè. Till today, the Babaláwo and the Olórìṣà present their sacrifices before Èṣù, and it gets accepted, with them seeing desired results.

Within the Yorùbá indigenous religion, Èṣù assumes a vital role and occupies a central position. In fact, no act of worship or sacrifice can be deemed acceptable to Olódumarè without being presented before Èṣù. However, the belief in the existence of Satan is prevalent across various cultures and societies worldwide. "Devil" is another term used to refer to Satan. In Hebrew, "Satan" means "adversary," while in Greek, "Devil" means "accuser." Satan personifies everything that opposes God. As a metaphysical being, Satan operates in the spiritual realm, coordinating his demons to oppose God's rule on earth and to antagonize human beings, who are considered the pinnacle of God's creation. In Christianity, Satan is believed to have been Lucifer, a bright and adorned morning star (Isaiah 14:12).

Irúnmọlẹ̀ (divinities) in Yorùbá land are beings believed to have emanated from the Supreme Being, their Creator. They serve and obey the Supreme Being. Some of these divinities are considered primordial, existing since the beginning. Others are deified ancestors or personifications of natural phenomena.

Satan is a figure primarily found in Abrahamic religions, particularly Christianity, Judaism, and Islam. Satan is often portrayed as a malevolent being who opposes God and tempts humans towards evil. Satan represents rebellion and temptation. Satan is seen as an enemy to both humanity and God. Due to his arrogance, he was expelled from heaven and has since wreaked havoc.

In Yorùbáland, Èṣù is a figure with a multifaceted personality and wide array of divine responsibilities. He is considered a divinity associated with moral uprightness, apprehending the wrongdoers, ensuring justice and serving the will of Olódumarè.

ÈŞÙ IS NOT SATAN

The arrival of Christianity and Islam in the religious landscape of the Yorùbá people had a profound impact on the perception and understanding of Èṣù. This divinity underwent significant changes, as different names and associations were attributed to him. Unfortunately, Èṣù became mistakenly linked to the concepts of the Devil or Shaytan found in these two religions' holy books. The notion that Èṣù is Satan or the author of all evils is false.

It is indeed wrong to equate Èṣù with the devil and the chief demon depicted in the New Testament of the Bible. It is unwelcomed to misconceive Èṣù as the embodiment of evil. Èṣù is neither the principal agent of darkness associated with witches and wizards, nor the chief demon among fallen angels, as presented in foreign theological beliefs. This misconception has caused significant harm to the true nature of Èṣù, who is a vassal of Olódumare.

Samuel Àjàyí Crowther, the first African Anglican Bishop, played a role in perpetuating this misconception. In his translation of the English Bible into Yorùbá around mid-19th century, Crowther erroneously drew parallels between Èṣù and Satan.

The translation of "Satan" in Yorùbá should be "Sátánì," as "Jesus Christ" was translated to "Jésù

Kristì" in the Yorùbá Bible.

In Yorùbá, Ọ̀rọ̀ Àyálò (Borrowed Words) are special words adopted by the Yorùbá native speakers from another language. Such adoption could be from English, Arabic and others to Yorùbá. Every language or society borrows one word or the other as its people interact closely. Example of such words from English to Yorùbá are Table - Tábílì, Bread - Búrẹ́dì, Tea - Tíì, Phone is fóónù, Ball - bọ́ọ̀lù, Television - Tẹlifísàn and others. Sátánì (coined and borrowed into Yorùbá from English) is the term to correctly represent Satan, especially since it does not have an origin or trace in the Yorùbá cosmology.

May Èṣù lead us towards goodness and bestow blessings upon us. Àṣẹ!